Florence Sabin
Teacher, Scientist, Humanitarian

Florence Sabin
Teacher, Scientist, Humanitarian

NOW YOU KNOW BIOS

Number Sixteen in the Series

E. E. Duncan

Filter Press, LLC
Palmer Lake, Colorado

Dedicated to the memory of my parents,
Lois and Ralph Shugart, in appreciation for the love of
learning they modeled throughout their lives,
and to Grandpa Wallace Guy Smeltzer
who loved history as much as I do.

ISBN: 978-0-86541-139-5
Library of Congress Control Number: 2014931860
Copyright © 2014 Elizabeth Duncan. All Rights Reserved.

Cover photo courtesy National Library of Medicine.

Florence Sabin: Teacher, Scientist, Humanitarian

Published by
Filter Press, LLC, P.O. Box 95, Palmer Lake, Colorado
719-481-2420 • info@FilterPressBooks.com

Printed in the United States of America

Contents

*Dr. Sabin and Governor Lee Knous on the day he signed
the Sabin Health Bills into law.*

Introduction

Florence Sabin accepted a pen from Colorado Governor Lee Knous. Moments before, he had used the pen to sign the Sabin Health Bills of 1947 into law. Her eyes sparkled and a smile of satisfaction spread across her wise, old face. At age 76, she had helped create a healthier future for Colorado.

The Sabin Health Laws were just one of Florence Sabin's accomplishments. Dr. Sabin had three separate and important careers—as a university **professor**, as a **research scientist**, and as a **public health advocate**. During her lifetime, she was called "the greatest living woman scientist."

At a time when most women did not go to college or have careers, Florence Sabin attended Smith College and Johns Hopkins University Medical School. Johns Hopkins was the first medical school to accept women on an equal basis with men. Florence was one of its first women graduates. She graduated at the top of her class. Her professors noticed her abilities in teaching and research.

Florence was so outstanding that Johns Hopkins Medical School hired her as their first woman professor. She taught classes in **anatomy** and **medical research**.

Later, Florence became famous for her work at The Rockefeller Institute for Medical Research in New York. As a research scientist, she made important discoveries about the causes and cures for disease. Her research focused on preventing a deadly lung disease called **tuberculosis**.

When she returned to Colorado, her childhood home, in 1938 she worked for better heath for all people. Colorado had one of the worst public health systems in the United States. Florence Sabin led a political fight to improve public health. The Sabin Laws ensured that Coloradans would have clean water, safe food, and better medical care.

In acknowledgment of her contribution to Colorado, a statue of Florence Sabin stands in the National Statuary Hall in the United States Capitol in Washington, DC. Each state is allowed two statues of distinguished persons. Florence Sabin and astronaut John Swigert represent Colorado.

*The statue of Florence Sabin in the US Capitol shows her with a
stack of books and her microscope at her side.*

1 A Colorado Girlhood

In the 1860s, Colorado Territory's Central City was a booming gold mining town. It was nestled in the aspens and pines of the beautiful Rocky Mountains, forty miles west of Denver. Gold had been discovered in Central City in 1859. Men poured into the area dreaming of striking it rich. Central City was called the "Richest Square Mile on Earth."

One of the hopeful miners was George Sabin who arrived in Central City in 1860. He had been a farmer and a medical student in Vermont. He set off in a wagon across the Great Plains to try his luck as a gold miner. George never struck it rich and soon took a job as a mine manager. He settled in Central City and became a town leader.

Courtesy Denver Public Library, Western History Collection, X-2656

The town of Central City was only nine years old when George and Rena Sabin were married there in 1868.

In 1865 a young schoolteacher named Serena "Rena" Miner, who had grown up in Vermont, moved to Central City. She arrived from Georgia by stage-coach to take a job teaching a handful of children in a one-room log schoolhouse.

Rena met George Sabin at a dance in 1868, and they married one month later. They settled in a two-story wooden house beside a steep road built into the side of a mountain. The house had one room down-stairs and a second room upstairs. In 1869 the couple

Courtesy Denver Public Library, Western History Collection, X-2703

*The Sabin family lived in this house in Central City from 1869
until they moved to Denver in 1875.*

had a baby girl they named Mary. Two years later, Florence Rena Sabin was born on November 9, 1871.

Florence and her older sister had happy memories of their life in Central City. As children they loved the outdoors and enjoyed walking in the hills and picking wildflowers. Long after they had moved from

Five-year-old
Florence Rena Sabin

Central City, they remembered the lovely sunsets, the rocky hills, and the mountain air of their childhoods. All her life, yellow was Florence's favorite color. It reminded her of the prickly pear cactus flowers and the wild roses that grew in Colorado's high country.

Central City was not a healthy place to live. Too many people lived in close and **unsanitary** conditions. The town had no running water. Water was delivered once a week by a truck and emptied into shared barrels. Illness and disease thrived in the mining camp.

Rena Sabin insisted on boiling the water her family used and scrubbing the house until it shone. These habits stayed with Florence all her life. Her interest in cleanliness as a way to promote health started at a very young age.

When Florence was four, the family moved to Denver. Florence's father traveled to the mining towns to conduct business. Denver was bustling with pioneers and gold miners headed to the mountains. At the edges of town, camps of Arapaho Indians lived in tepees. It was an unsettled and rough place.

The family lived in a brick house in downtown Denver. The girls played in the dusty dirt streets. Mary started school at Broadway School, the local public school. Their mother, a former teacher, taught her girls to read and to add and subtract long before they were enrolled in school. When Florence entered school the year after the move to Denver, she was already ahead of her classmates.

Mary and Florence had very different personalities. Mary was outgoing and friendly. Florence, on the other hand, was a shy, quiet girl who did not make friends easily. Florence depended on her sister to help her make friends and enjoy the company of others.

The sisters were very close friends in childhood and throughout their lives.

In 1876 a baby brother named Richman was born. The girls were delighted with the newest addition to the family. When Richman died before his first birthday, the entire family grieved. Then a year later, another baby boy, Albert, was born.

The family was happy until it became clear that Florence's mother had become deathly ill. Rena Sabin died on Florence's seventh birthday. As an adult, Florence remembered, "The day my mother died was the last day of my childhood."

George Sabin was overwhelmed with sadness. He had three children to care for and needed to work long days at his mining business. He could not manage by himself. He decided to send baby Albert to live with his sister in Central City. He enrolled Mary and Florence in Wolfe Hall, a Denver **boarding school**. Florence was grief stricken over the deaths in the family, and she hated boarding school. She dreamed of living at home with her family. That was not to be. When little Albert died the next year, the family was shattered. The girls never lived with their father again.

Denver around 1870. Wolfe Hall, where Florence and Mary attended school, is the three-story building in the upper right.

2 Finding a Family

George Sabin knew his girls needed a stable home. When they were nine and eleven, he arranged for them to move to Chicago, Illinois. They lived with their Uncle Albert and his family for the next four years.

Uncle Albert was a schoolteacher who welcomed his nieces into his household. Florence, who was very shy, became close to her uncle. They shared a love of reading, math, and music. Uncle Albert was proud of his intelligent nieces. He encouraged them to develop their minds.

Florence learned to play the piano that sat in the front parlor of the Chicago home. She had musical talent, and with hard work and determination, she flourished as a pianist. Playing the piano was a great comfort to the lonely girl.

Know More!

Florence's Uncle Albert wrote this recipe for happiness. Uncle Albert helped raise Florence and her sister. He sent the recipe to Florence in a Christmas letter when she was ten years old.

In a creative way, the recipe shows the Sabin family values of hard work and caring for others. Florence kept the recipe and treasured it all her life.

Our Sabin Family Recipe

To absolute purity, add a wise mixture of parts,
Not too much of this or too little of that.
Stir well with a clear conscience and a wooden spoon.
Boil gently over a fire made of happy labor and a few coals.
When at just the right temperature, set away to cool,
But not until you have put into it the best of yourself
and flavored it with goodwill for everyone.

Write your own family recipe. Use ingredients that reflect the values of your family.

The Sabin girls visited their grandparents in Vermont each summer. Grandfather and Grandmother Sabin lived in a little white farmhouse surrounded by rocky wooded hills. Florence loved spending time outdoors. She took long hikes, observing and identifying flowers, birds, and wildlife.

Courtesy, National Library of Medicine

When Florence was fourteen, she and Mary moved from
Chicago to Vermont to live with grandparents. This photograph
was made while Florence was a student at Vermont Academy
in Saxtons River, Vermont.

Florence learned from her Grandmother Sabin
that her father had studied to be a doctor before he left
the East for Colorado. Other Sabin relatives had been
doctors, too. "It's too bad you're not a boy. You
would have made a good doctor," her grandmother
told her.

When Florence was fourteen, she and Mary moved
to Vermont to live year round with their grandparents.

They attended Vermont Academy, an excellent school for girls. When their grandmother died the following winter, the girls moved to the academy to live. Florence lived at the school until her graduation at age 18.

Uncle Albert bought a piano for Florence to keep at school. Florence spent hours and hours practicing. She dreamed she would grow up to be a concert pianist and earn a living playing piano for large audiences. Later, she began to have doubts about her abilities. After years of practicing and lessons, she gave up playing the piano. She decided to focus instead on her abilities in science and math.

Florence spent her final two years at Vermont Academy taking the hardest classes that the school offered. She did well in all subjects, but she excelled in science. Although she was quiet and reserved, her classmates elected her president of the senior class. They appreciated and rewarded her academic ability. She graduated from the Academy with honors.

Despite her success at school, Florence had made few friends in her years at Vermont Academy. Florence was still painfully shy and disliked the casual conversations of her classmates. She longed to be with her sister Mary, who enjoyed talking about challenging ideas, literature, and current events.

Mary, who was two years ahead of Florence in school, was enrolled at Smith College for Women in Northampton, Massachusetts. After her graduation from Vermont Academy, Florence looked forward to joining Mary at Smith College.

3 Smith College

Mary worried about how well her quiet, studious sister would fit into college life. She arranged for Florence to live with her at Mrs. Tenney's **boarding house**. She decorated their room in yellow because it was Florence's favorite color.

Florence enjoyed the challenge of classes and the academic focus of college. Plus, she loved living with her sister again. They took long walks around the beautiful Smith campus and roamed the woods on nature walks.

The sisters remained very different. Mary liked attending parties and going out on dates. Florence preferred to stay in the boarding house with a good book for company. Florence enjoyed intellectual discussions and could not tolerate chit-chat and small talk.

In the 1890s, most colleges were only for male students. Smith College was founded to provide young women the opportunity for advanced learning. The professors at Smith tried to inspire in their students "the wish to know."

Florence nurtured her own "wish to know." She had a curious and creative mind, and she sought new challenges to explore. Her coursework at Smith included philosophy, literature, religion, mathematics, science, and languages. Florence continued to have a passion for science. She spent many hours in the laboratory conducting experiments.

Florence was invited to join a science club called the **Colloquium**. At club meetings, members presented scientific papers and discussed scientific theories and ideas. This was the kind of conversation Florence enjoyed. While it was a serious club, the young women also had some fun. They had "tea parties" in the science classroom where they drank from **beakers** and stirred their tea with test tubes.

In her junior year, Florence took a zoology class. *Zoology* is the scientific study of animals. She was fascinated by **dissection** of animals and learning how animal bodies worked. She decided that zoology would be her **major**. She earned the respect of her professors by her work in the laboratory and received high grades and honors.

Florence wondered what she might do when she graduated. Most young women married and became mothers and homemakers. Florence was not interested in getting married.

Florence thought she might want to become a doctor. She spoke to Dr. Grace Preston, the woman doctor on the staff at Smith College. Dr. Preston explained that there were few women doctors, and women physicians were not always accepted. Becoming a doctor would be a challenge and would mean years of hard work and intense study. She might also face **discrimination** as a woman doctor. Florence was not discouraged. She started to dream of the challenge of medical school.

Johns Hopkins University Medical School opened in 1893—the same year Florence graduated from Smith College. The medical school had an unusual admissions policy. Johns Hopkins was the first medical school in the United States to admit women on the same terms as men.

Women were admitted to the medical school because some wealthy women in Baltimore, Maryland, provided the money to start the medical school. They told the university they would give the money to build a medical school only if women were admitted. All applicants, male and female, needed a college degree and knowledge of physics, chemistry, biology, and foreign languages. With her Smith College education and grades, Florence was a strong applicant to Hopkins.

Florence in 1893, the year she graduated from Smith College.

Courtesy National Library of Medicine

In spite of this, Florence could not enter the first medical school class at Johns Hopkins University. Her father's mining business was not going well. Her sister, Mary, had moved back to Denver to work as a math teacher in Denver Public Schools. She made very little money as a teacher. Florence and her family could not afford the medical school tuition.

Florence remained determined to attend medical school. For the next three years, Florence and her family worked to earn money to pay her tuition.

Florence took a job teaching high school at Wolfe Hall, the school she and Mary had attended after their mother died. At first Florence was worried that she was too shy to teach high school students. She soon found that she enjoyed teaching. She had a lot of knowledge to share. Florence wanted to inspire in her students "the wish to know" that the Smith professors had inspired in her. On Saturdays she led nature hikes for students to explore the outdoors.

The enthusiastic young teacher caught the interest of the Denisons, a wealthy couple whose children attended Wolfe Hall. The family invited Florence and Mary to spend the summer with them at Lake Geneva, near Chicago. For two summers, the sisters taught science and an appreciation of nature to the Dension's children.

Mrs. Ella Dension eventually became an important part of Florence and Mary's lives. The Denison children stayed in touch with "dear Miss Florence" for the rest of their lives. She was like a beloved aunt to them.

During the summer days, the sisters led their

students in studies of nature and science through observation. They watched tadpoles turn into frogs and dissected flowers to identify their parts. The evenings were filled with conversation, music, and games.

Florence remembered the summers she spent at Lake Geneva as some of the happiest times of her life. The shy and solitary Florence was developing a new confidence in herself and her abilities. She and Mary returned often to visit the family in the lovely cabin in

Wolfe Hall, where Florence was a student and returned to teach in 1893, was located at 17th and Champa Streets in Denver.

the Illinois woods. The Densions accepted the sisters as part of their family.

Florence taught for two years at Wolfe Hall. Then she taught zoology at Smith College for another year. Finally, three years after graduating from college, Florence and her family had saved enough money for her to attend medical school. She applied and was accepted to Johns Hopkins University Medical School. At twenty-five years old, Florence became a member of the class that would graduate in 1900.

4 Medical School

Florence entered Johns Hopkins University Medical School in 1896. Of the forty-two students in her class, fourteen were women. It was no longer so unusual to be a woman in medical school. She and her first year classmates took anatomy, biochemistry, physiology, pharmacology, and bacteriology. They worked long hours on their class work. They spent time in the laboratories conducting experiments. Florence showed unusual talent for using a **microscope** efficiently.

One professor, Dr. Franklin Mall, was passionately interested in research. He saw in Florence an ability to conduct research that he called "one in ten-thousand." Florence had the patience, attention to detail, and creativity needed to excel at laboratory work. Dr. Mall became Florence's **mentor** during her years at Hopkins, He encouraged her interest in research and helped her develop her research abilities.

Years later Florence said, "I had an idea that I would come back to Colorado and work as a lady doctor. I think that was the only idea anyone had of medicine at that time." However, opportunities were expanding. The late 1890s was the beginning of modern medical research. She said, "I lived through the most marvelous period in the development of medicine. I was part of the very beginning of medical research in this country."

When Florence was in her second year of medical school, Dr. Mall assigned her an exciting research project. He asked her to study the human **lymphatic system**. She discovered a new way to stain cells with special ink that made cells easier to see under the microscope. Because of this, she discovered new information about the lymphatic system. She wrote and published papers. She was given an award "for the best scientific paper written by a woman in independent laboratory research."

Florence sent a copy of her award to her father back in Colorado. Sadly, he died before he saw it. Florence traveled to Denver for his funeral during her

Christmas holiday break in 1898. She and Mary spent Christmas together before Florence headed back to school. Although Mary and Florence went on many summertime adventures together, they would not spend another Christmas together until they retired forty years later.

In the second year of medical school, students focused on disease. Florence continued to excel in class. Dr. Mall challenged her with interesting projects and ideas. She was fascinated to learn how disease affects the body. She studied surgery and practiced by operating on animals.

In their third year, the medical students began working with patients. Poor people came to the medical school for low-cost treatment. Florence saw how illness and disease affected people. She wished that she could do more to help her patients, but too little was known about what caused diseases. Florence wanted to help *prevent* disease, rather than just treating a disease after a patient had it.

Dr. Mall asked Florence to make a model of the brain of a newborn baby. This project had never been done before. She created a three-dimensional model out of hard, colored wax. It showed the complicated

Courtesy National Library of Medicine

Dr. Franklin Mall helped Florence become an adept researcher. He guided her early career.

bundles of cells and nerve fibers at the base of the brain. Her model helped doctors better understand the brain. Other medical schools used copies of the model to teach their students.

Florence started another project about the brain. She wrote a book about the structure of the human brain entitled, *An Atlas of the Medulla and Midbrain.* She included drawings of the brain and described how the brain worked. The book was so well done, it was used as a textbook for medical students. It can still be found in medical libraries today.

During her fourth year, Florence decided not to become a practicing doctor. In order to graduate, medical students had to deliver nine babies. Florence did *not* enjoy delivering babies. She wrote to Mary, "I find I don't seem to work well under pressure. I need a calm and placid environment." It was research, not treating patients, that Florence decided to make her career. At the end of her senior year, when she had to declare a specialty, Florence chose medical research.

In order to finish their medical training, the graduates needed to complete a one-year internship at a hospital. Only the top students were offered internships at Johns Hopkins Hospital. Florence was among the top students, but because she was a woman, she had to fight to be allowed to complete her training at the hospital. Then, after the internship was complete, the hospital would not allow a woman to be a teacher in the medical school. Florence was experiencing discrimination. She was not given the job simply because she was a woman.

Instead, Florence accepted a fellowship as a researcher in Dr. Mall's laboratory where she continued her work on the lymphatic system. She did outstanding work, published her findings, and became better known in the medical community.

The 1900 Johns Hopkins University School of Medicine graduating class.
Florence Sabin is standing on the far left in the photograph.

5 Professor Sabin

In 1902, when Florence was 31 years old, Johns Hopkins Medical School offered her a job as assistant instructor of anatomy. Fifteen years later, in 1917, she became the first woman to be promoted to full professor at Johns Hopkins School of Medicine. Her accomplishments were so outstanding that the university changed its policy against women teachers. In her new job, Florence would be able to teach and conduct research. These were her favorite activities. Florence worked as a professor and medical researcher at Hopkins for the next twenty-three years.

The summer before she began teaching at Hopkins, Florence traveled to Europe. Mary joined her for the trip. The sisters would often travel together over the decades that followed. They filled their days with sightseeing, attending lectures and concerts, and shopping. In a letter from Paris, Florence wrote, "I have a new hat and dress...and what do you think—underclothes with lace and pink ribbons!"

Florence returned to Baltimore and began her career at Johns Hopkins. She taught anatomy and research methods to first-year medical students. She had much knowledge and enthusiasm to share with her students. Over the years, she became an outstanding **lecturer**. After each lecture, Florence destroyed her

Professor Sabin at Johns Hopkins University School of Medicine.

notes. She wanted each year's lectures to be fresh and up-to-date.

She followed the advice of Dr. Mall, who told her to "give students the pleasure of discovering things for themselves." Florence encouraged her students to ask questions and helped them find the answers through research. Like Dr. Mall, she gave her students real medical problems. She pushed her students to conduct original and meaningful research.

In addition Florence conducted her own research. She published her findings in medical journals. Most of her work focused on the lymphatic system and she made important discoveries. The papers she wrote had long scientific titles such as, "Further Evidence on the Origin of the Lymphatic Endothelium from Endothelium of the Blood Vascular System."

Because Florence had spent years studying the lymphatic system, she was sensitive about her research. When others questioned her findings, she felt very insulted. She had great confidence in her work. She stood up to her critics and became well known in her field of medical research. When she complained about the criticism, Uncle Albert wrote to her, "I think you are grand. Your old uncle will love you still and believe you the best of the pack."

Florence's life in Baltimore centered on her work at Johns Hopkins. She also found time to enjoy herself. After years of living in **dormitories** and boarding houses, she rented a lovely apartment near the medical school. She decorated the apartment in yellow and kept it sparkling clean.

Florence became a loyal baseball fan, cheering on the Baltimore Orioles with fierce devotion. Florence began to collect art. She enjoyed classical music concerts and supporting the arts.

Florence also gave fabulous dinner parties. Because she hated small talk, she sent her guests a list of discussion topics before the party. She also asked them to help prepare the food and wrote instructions about their part in the meal. When the party was over, she boiled the dishes to kill germs.

Florence and Mary went on adventure after adventure on their summer breaks from school. The sisters sailed to Alaska, climbed mountains in Europe, and drove a Model A car through the Rockies. They went on a two-month walking tour through the Italian Alps. Florence wrote this to a friend about a car trip to Yellowstone, "It was a great adventure, over awful

Know More!

The Other Miss Sabin

Mary Sabin, Florence's older sister, also contributed to Colorado. Like Florence, she never married. She enjoyed being single and independent.

After she graduated from Smith College, Mary returned to Denver. She taught mathematics for forty years at East High School in the Denver Public Schools. When she was hired in 1891, she was the only teacher at the school with a college degree. She was a very strict teacher and enjoyed challenging each of her students.

Mary was the first woman in Denver to own and drive a car. She attended auto mechanics classes at Emily Griffith's Opportunity School and learned to repair the car herself.

Mary loved mountain climbing and organized hiking trips to places all over the world. She heard about mountain clubs while she was in Switzerland climbing in the Alps. She started the Colorado Mountain Club in 1913. With other club members, Mary climbed Colorado's mountains, including many more than 14,000 feet high. The club continues to offer outdoor activities to hundreds of members today.

roads and we had every difficulty—except we didn't run over anyone or tip over! We got stuck in snow and mud, and wore out tires and gears. I now know all about the anatomy of a car!"

Florence also developed deep and lasting friendships. The shy, friendless girl had grown to value having close friends. Florence became like a sister to Dr. Mall and his wife, Mabel, and like an aunt to their children.

Doctors Edith and Donald Hooker were another set of close friends. They had attended medical

Courtesy, National Library of Medicine

Mary Sabin during the years she taught at Denver's East High School.

school with Florence. The Hookers were committed to improving public health. They started a home for single mothers and established free healthcare clinics. Florence spent many Christmases in their busy household of eight children and ten dogs.

Florence enjoyed discussing politics with famous author Gertrude Stein and her brother Leo. The three friends often attended arts events and took road trips together.

Back in Colorado, Florence continued her friendship with the large Denison family. Ella Denison wrote and visited Florence often. Mrs. Denison was like a mother to Florence, helping her with hard decisions and giving her advice. Two of the Denison children grew up to become Florence's students at Johns Hopkins Medical School.

Florence's friends—Mabel Mall, Dr. Edith Hooker, and Gertrude Stein—were active in the **suffrage** movement. They worked to change the nation's laws so that women would have the right to vote. Florence was too busy to take an active role in the **women's rights movement**, but she supported the idea with all her heart. Florence believed that by working hard and proving that a woman could be an outstanding scientist, she was doing her part for women's rights. Women were finally allowed to vote in 1920—twenty years after Florence became a doctor.

When Dr. Mall died in 1917, Florence was the logical choice to replace him as **chairman** of the Johns Hopkins Anatomy Department. Instead, a man was chosen for the position. Once again, Florence experienced discrimination. She was denied opportunity for no reason other than she was a woman. Florence was upset and thought about leaving Johns Hopkins. In the end, she decided to stay because she "had research in progress."

Florence's reputation continued to grow. She began to win honors. She was awarded an **honorary doctorate** of science from Smith College. Seventeen other colleges awarded her the same honor. She became the first woman president of the American Association of Anatomists. In 1924 she was the first woman elected to the National Academy of Sciences. Florence always remained humble and grateful for the attention she received.

She continued to publish her research and present papers at medical conventions. She still loved teaching and enjoyed the challenge of her own research. Florence might have been happy to live in Baltimore and teach at Johns Hopkins for the rest of her career, but another opportunity came to her.

The Rockefeller Institute in New York City asked her to join the research team there. After twenty-three years working at Johns Hopkins, Florence accepted a new job.

On May 1, 1925, the *Baltimore Sun* newspaper printed a front-page article about their famous woman scientist leaving Baltimore for a new job in New York City.

6 The Foremost Woman Scientist

John D. Rockefeller was American's richest man in the early 1900s. He made his money in the oil business. One of Mr. Rockefeller's grandsons had died of **scarlet fever.** He decided to use some of his fortune to find cures for deadly diseases. In 1901 he started The Rockefeller Institute for Medical Research in New York City. The Institute was based on the idea that science could and should benefit humanity.

At the age of fifty-four, Florence took charge of a new department at The Rockefeller Institute. It was called the Department of Cellular Studies. She was the first woman to be hired as a head researcher at The Rockefeller Institute. The research goal at the department was to find a cure for tuberculosis. Tuberculosis was a major cause of death in America.

Florence loved her work. Her department focused on studying blood. The work required long hours of peering into a microscope, counting blood cells, and recording her observations. Fortunately, attention to detail and patience were Florence's strengths. She wrote in a New Year's Day letter to Mary, "I hope you have had as nice a day as I have had. I went over to the laboratory and spent the day with my little [microscopic] friends."

Florence was strict with her employees. She insisted everyone's research be flawless. But she also created a pleasant work environment. She was enthusiastic and passionate about her own research. Her eyes sparkled when she talked about her work.

Florence Sabin and her researchers did not find the cure for tuberculosis. No one scientist found the cure for tuberculosis. The cure was found through the contributions of many scientists studying the disease. Florence understood that slow and steady gathering of information and knowledge would lead to the discovery of a cure.

Florence wrote to her sister, "Life in New York is truly a great adventure!" The Rockefeller Institute paid their researchers well. Florence's days of scrimping and saving money were over. While she was not extravagant, she enjoyed the advantages of living in the nation's largest city.

She rented a bright, sunny apartment in a high-rise building and decorated it in her favorite color—yellow. She filled it with art and books. As she had in Baltimore, she hosted lovely dinner parties where the art of good conversation was required. She attended cultural events such as plays, concerts, ballets, and operas.

Florence was invited to become a member of the Cosmopolitan Club. This was a private women's club

Courtesy History Colorado, F-2242

Florence Sabin at The Rockefeller Institute doing what she liked best, peering into a microscope.

where members gathered to "nourish their intellects, exercise their artistic impulses, cultivate friends, and freely exchange ideas."

She had learned to love baseball in Baltimore. She now had a new favorite team—the Brooklyn Dodgers. When she could not attend games she listened to them on the radio. On the weekends, she enjoyed making jelly and preserves and baking sweets for her co-workers.

Florence served on boards of hospitals and health related charities. She was often asked to speak at events. No longer shy, she enjoyed talking to groups about her work. She maintained her sweet, modest character, and always seemed a little surprised at the attention she received.

Florence became the best-known woman scientist in America. She had already received many academic awards. Now she started to receive non-academic awards. The National Women's Party named her as one of the "World's Twelve Greatest Living Women" in 1923. *Good Housekeeping* magazine selected her as one of the "Twelve Most Eminent American Women" in 1931.

The *Pictorial Review* awarded her the "Most Distinctive Contribution in the Field of Arts, Science and Letters." *Time* magazine claimed Florence had "one on the keenest scientific brains in the world." In 1935 her photograph was on the cover of *Medical Women's Journal,* along with an article about her research.

At a special award ceremony at Bryn Mawr College, the college president said, "We believe you to be the foremost woman among American investigators in science." President Herbert Hoover invited her to dine at the White House at a special dinner honoring scientists. When the Nobel Prize-winning French scientist Madame Marie Curie visited America, Florence had the honor of introducing her to the American Association of University Women. Another time she sat next to the famous German scientist Albert Einstein at an honorary dinner.

After thirteen years at The Rockefeller Institute, Florence decided it was time to retire. She was sixty-seven years old and had some health problems. Mary wanted her to return to Colorado. Mary had retired from her career as a teacher in the Denver Public Schools, and she urged Florence to come home.

Her New York friends gave her a surprise retirement party at the famous Rainbow Room restaurant at Rockefeller Center in New York City. Her friends and co-workers bid her a fond farewell. They spoke lovingly of her and of her achievements in science and her contributions to their lives.

Florence did not want to retire. But she recognized that she it was time and that she needed to make room for young scientists and their new ideas. When she left The Rockefeller Institute, she donated her Spencer microscope to the lab. Her microscope was a state-of-

Know More!

The Sabin Polio Vaccine

A research scientist named Albert Sabin, who was not related to Florence, developed the Sabin polio **vaccine** in 1952. Polio is an infectious desease that killed and crippled people before a vaccine was developed.

Albert Sabin and Florence both worked at The Rockefeller Institute for Medical Research in the 1930s. They spent their careers researching cures for diseases. They probably knew each other and likely admired each other's work.

the-art scientific instrument and a treasured personal possession.

The *New York Times* interviewed her at the time of her retirement. She was asked about the most exciting moment of her life. Florence did not refer to any award or honor. Always the scientist, she answered, "The most exciting moment was when I witnessed [under a microscope] the birth of the first blood cells in the embryo of a chick and first saw the beat of its heart."

7 A War on Rats and Dirty Milk

Florence left New York City in 1938 and returned to Denver. Mary had retired from teaching school five years earlier. "It's high time you resigned!" she wrote to Florence. Neither woman had married, and they had long dreamed of setting up a home together. For the next six years, Florence traveled, conducted research, and lectured. Then, a new opportunity presented itself.

In 1944, when Florence was seventy-three years old, Colorado Governor John Vivian asked her to serve on a committee studying health issues in Colorado. The committee was officially named the Health Committee of the Governor of Colorado's Post-War Planning Committee. The governor did not want to change health laws. He believed that a "little old lady scientist" would not fight for change.

Florence surprised the governor by taking charge of the committee and taking the work very seriously.

Florence and her committee first examined Colorado's current health records. They learned that Colorado had one of the worst health records in the United States! Four Coloradans died each day from preventable disease.

Sewage was dumped into streams, drinking water was polluted, and town dumps were breeding grounds for horrible diseases. Rats roamed the trashy alleyways of the cities, and beef and dairy products from sick cows spread disease.

Florence knew these health problems could be fixed if Colorado had laws that required better sanitation and pure drinking water. Colorado also needed more laws on food production—laws that required pasteurized milk and meat free of disease. Florence said, "I've started a war on flies, rats, and dirty milk."

The committee thought that more could be done to prevent disease. Children needed medical checkups and free **immunizations**. Florence wanted to provide free x-rays to test people for tuberculosis. Colorado needed more hospitals and clinics to treat sick people and prevent the spread of disease. The state needed

Florence set an example for others by having a chest x-ray. An important part of public health is finding sick people who may not know they have a disease. X-rays helped health workers find people who had tuberculosis.

more doctors and better research facilities.

The committee published a report that listed fourteen **health bills** they wanted the state legislature to make into laws. The report went to Governor Vivian. The committee was afraid he would ignore it, so they printed and handed out 1,000 copies. Florence said, "It's hard to put 1,000 copies in a desk drawer!"

Florence hosted dinners at Denver's famous Brown Palace Hotel. She invited important people and told them about Colorado's health problems. She convinced them that changes had to be made to Colorado's health laws.

She also invited owners in the beef and dairy industry to dinners at "the Brown." The meat and dairy farmers were afraid that the Sabin Health Bills would cost them money. She told them that having healthier cows would make them *more* money. Their dairy cows would give more milk, the cows would live longer, and more calves would live. Their beef cows would be bigger and produce more meat.

Then, she took her message to the people of Colorado. Seventy-five-year-old Florence traveled all over Colorado, telling ordinary people about the state's health problems. In a little pink leaflet titled "Basic Heath Needs of Colorado," she outlined the Sabin Health Bills. She went to PTA meetings, churches, community centers, and town halls. She wanted the people of Colorado to elect for politicians who would vote to make the Sabin Health Bills into new laws.

Florence was passionate about improving health care, and her energy seemed unlimited. One supporter

Know More!

By speaking to groups large and small all over Colorado and giving out thousands of brochures entitled, "Basic Health Needs of Colorado," Florence educated Coloradans about the health problems in the state. Among the basic public health changes called for were pasteurization of milk, safe drinking water, and sanitary sewage systems throughout the state.

Why were pasteurization and sewage systems important to everyone's health? Look at a milk carton in your refrigerator. Does it state that the milk has been pasteurized? For extra challenge, research the origins and meaning of the word *pasteurization*.

called her "a sweet, lovable tornado!" Health became a central issue of the 1946 governor's race. Candidate Lee Knous supported the Sabin Health Bills as part of his campaign. He said, "When it comes to the Health Bills, there isn't a man in the government that wants to tangle with her. She's an atom bomb!" Lee Knous was elected in a **landslide.** Other candidates who supported the health bills were also elected. The Sabin Health Bills were passed into law in 1947.

Within two years, the number of cases of tuberculosis in Colorado was cut in half. There were fewer deaths from **diphtheria, typhoid,** and **influenza**—all

contagious diseases. Babies and children were healthier and so were their parents. Modern sewage and water treatment plants were built all over Colorado. Milk was made safer. Beef products were tested for disease. New hospitals, clinics, and research facilities were built.

Although Florence was busy, she kept learning. She continued to read medical journals and kept up with developments in medical research. She read all of Shakespeare's plays as well as many modern books. She belonged to a woman's group that studied literature together. She and her sister made weekly trips to the Denver Public Library to check out stacks of books.

Florence and Mary loved the Colorado mountains and took short hikes and drives through the Rockies. They played a card game called canasta with friends every week. The sisters played as a team and often beat their friends.

They decorated their Capitol Hill apartment with art, books, and Oriental rugs. Their home was cozy, as well as clean and tidy. Florence loved baseball, and Mary was an avid football fan. On weekends, they attended Denver East High School's baseball and football games. Florence still enjoyed cooking, but she was busier than ever and did not have as many dinner parties.

The City of Denver asked Florence to be the head of Denver's new health department. She accepted and for the next five years, from the time she was 76 to age 80, she worked for Denver's Board of Health and Hospitals. To support health research, she donated her salary to the University of Colorado Medical Center. She also wrote articles about public health so that other states could improve their health care laws as the voters in Colorado had done.

8 The Final Years

In 1951 Florence was at last ready to *really* retire. That year the University of Colorado dedicated the Florence Rena Sabin Building for Research in Cellular Biology. A scholarship for women who worked in public heath was set up in her name.

The *Denver Post* published an article for Florence's eightieth birthday. The headline read, "Dr. Sabin on Eve of 80—She's Busy with a Half-Dozen Jobs That Need Doing!" Like many other articles, it mentioned her "blue eyes sparkling and crackling with electricity" when she spoke about public health and other issues.

Mary became very ill, and Florence took care of her. Mary was losing her memory, as well as having physical problems. Eventually, Mary needed full-time care in a nursing home.

Florence Sabin's favorite poem was "The Bridge Builder." She kept a copy over her desk and quoted it in her speeches. The poem is about an old man who decides to build a bridge for the young people who come after him.

Read the poem aloud and listen for the quiet rhythm and rhymes. For an extra challenge, memorize the poem.

Why do you think that Dr. Sabin liked the poem? Does the poem have more to do with her life as a teacher or more to do with her life as a researcher?

The Bridge Builder

An old man going a lone highway
Came at evening cold and gray
To a chasm, vast and deep and wide
Through which was flowing a sullen tide.

The old man crossed in the twilight dim
The sullen stream had no fears for him
But he turned when safe on the other side
And built a bridge to span the tide.

"Old man," said a fellow pilgrim near,
"You're wasting your strength with building here.
Your journey will end with the ending day
You never again will pass this way.
You've crossed the chasm, deep and wide,
Why build you this bridge at eventide?"

The builder lifted his old, gray head.
"Good friend, in the path I have come," he said,
"There followed after me today
A youth whose feet must pass this way.

This chasm that has been naught to me
To that fair-haired youth may a pitfall be;
He, too, must cross in the twilight dim.
Good friend, I am building this bridge for him."

— Will Allen Dromgoole

Florence herself became ill with pneumonia and spent some time in the hospital. In the fall of 1953, she was well enough to come home from the hospital.

On October 3, 1953, the World Series was on television. Florence still loved baseball. Her favorite team, the Brooklyn Dodgers, was losing 5 to 4 to the New York Yankees. As she did in all the games, Florence stood at the end of the seventh inning to stretch. Florence fell to the floor. She had died of a heart attack at the age of 82.

Her death was front-page news in the Denver newspapers. People came from all over the United States to attend a simple funeral held at St. John's Cathedral in Denver. Mayor Quigg Newton spoke at her funeral. He said, "Dr. Sabin was one of the greatest persons I've ever known. She was learned, she was wise, she was humble. She loved the world and every living creature in it."

9   Florence's Legacy

In her will, Florence made sure that Mary would be cared for. Mary died two years after Florence. Florence arranged to have all her remaining money donated to the University of Colorado School of Medicine. The money was to be used for research and educational activities.

After the sisters died, Denver Public Schools named Sabin Elementary School in their honor. In Colorado Springs, Sabin Middle School was named for Dr. Sabin, as were several other schools in the United States.

In 1956 a women's group in Loveland, Colorado, had the idea to put a statue of Florence Sabin in the National Statuary Hall in the US Capitol in Washington, DC. Each state is allowed two statues, and in 1956, Colorado did not have even one. Over the next four years, groups and individuals raised $25,000 to have the statue built. A woman sculptor named Joy Buba was hired to create the large bronze statue with a marble base.

Florence is one of six women and one of only four doctors honored in Statuary Hall. The statue is unusual in the pose. It shows Florence seated at a desk with her arm resting on a stack of books and a microscope beside her. The inscription reads:

Florence Rena Sabin 1871–1953
Doctor of Medicine
Teacher, Scientist, Humanitarian

Know More!

Florence Sabin's philosophy of life was summarized in her book plate. What was her philosophy? How does the microscope reflect her philosophy? Who was Leonardo da Vinci? What does *Ex libris* mean? Make a guess at the meaning of *dost*. Is *labour* a misspelling? Can you guess the meaning of *Thou*? Create a bookplate for your own books.

Timeline

November 9, 1871 — Florence Rena Sabin was born in Central City, Colorado.

1875 — Sabin family moved to Denver, Colorado.

1878 — Florence's mother died.

1880 — Florence and Mary moved to Chicago to live with their uncle. They spent summers in Vermont with grandparents.

1885–1889 — Florence attended Vermont Academy.

1889–1893 — Florence attended Smith College.

1893–1895 — Florence taught at Wolfe Hall.

1895–1896 — Returned to Smith College to teach zoology.

1896–1900 — Attended Johns Hopkins University School of Medicine.

1901–1925 — Florence conducted research on the lymphatic system and brain at Johns Hopkins.

1902 — Florence began teaching anatomy at Johns Hopkins.

1917 — Appointed Professor of Histology at Johns Hopkins.

1925 — Florence became the first woman elected to National Academy of Sciences.

1925–1938 — Moved to New York City to head the Department of Cellular Studies at The Rockefeller Institute.

1938 — Florence retired and moved to Colorado.

1944 — Florence was appointed chair of the Colorado Committee on Health.

1944–1947 — Campaigned across Colorado for adoption of the Sabin Health Bills.

1947 — The Colorado legislature passed the Sabin Health Bills.

1947–1951 — Florence served as chair of the Board of Health and Hospitals of Denver.

October 3, 1953 — Florence Sabin died in Denver.

1959 — A statue of Florence was placed in the National Statuary Hall in the US Capitol.

Glossary

Anatomy – the branch of science that studies the physical structure of animals

Boarding house – a private house where rooms and meals are provided to paying guests

Boarding school – a school where students live

Chairman – a member of a university staff who is in charge of an academic department

Colloquium – an academic gathering in which a particular topic is discussed

Contagious – able to be spread by contact between individuals

Diphtheria – a serious disease that damages the heart and nervous system

Discrimination – unfair treatment of a person because of their race, ethnic group, age, religion, or gender

Dissection – the cutting and separating of the parts of animals or plants for scientific study

Dormitories – buildings in which college students live

Health bills – a proposal for new laws related to health care

Histology – the branch of science that studies the microscopic structures of animal and plant tissue

Honorary doctorate – an honor given by universities to individuals to recognize their contributions to a field of study

Immunizations – treatments, often with an injected vaccine, that produce immunity or resistance to a disease

Influenza (flu) – a serious disease with fever, exhaustion, severe aches and pains, and inflammation of the respiratory tract

Landslide – an overwhelming victory in an election

Lecturer – someone who gives an informative speech on a particular topic

Lymphatic system – the network of vessels that transport fluid, fats, and proteins to the bloodstream and removes microorganisms from tissues

Major – a specialty area of study selected for a college degree

Medical research – the investigation of a medical problem to discover facts, establish or revise a theory, or to develop a plan of action based on the facts

Mentor – a person, usually older and more experienced, who provides advice and support to a less experienced person

Professor – a teacher in a college or university

Public health advocate – a person who works for the improvement of community health through preventive medicine and improving sanitation

Research scientist – a person who investigates a theory to discover facts, or a plan of action based on new facts

Suffrage – the right to vote

Tuberculosis – a serious disease that affects the lungs and the ability to breathe

Typhoid – a disease that causes fever, diarrhea, weakness, and headache, and is passed from one person to another in contaminated food or water

Vaccine – a substance injected or given by mouth to protect an individual against a particular disease

Women's rights movement – the work of people to assure that women had the same rights as men, including the right to vote

Bibliography

Bluemel, Elinor. *Florence Sabin: Colorado Woman of the Century*. University of Colorado Press: Boulder, Colorado, 1959.

Bluemel, Elinor. Papers, manuscripts and letters, 1903 - 1974. Denver Public Library, Western History & Genealogy Department.

Campbell, Robin. *Florence Sabin, Scientist* (Junior World Biographies Series.) Chelsea House Publishers: New York, 1995.

Florence R. Sabin Papers. Sophia Smith Collection: Smith College.

History Learning Site. "First World War Casualties," http://www.historylearningsite.co.uk/FWWcasualties.htm

Kaye, Judith. *The Life of Florence Sabin* (Pioneers in Health and Medicine Series). Henry Holt: New York, 1993.

Phelan, Mary Kay. *Probing the Unknown: The Story of Dr. Florence Sabin*. Crowell Company: New York, 1969.

Sabin, Florence. Oral History: Radio Interviews, October 25, 1951 and November 11, 1951. Denver Public Library: Western History/ Genealogy Department.

Shirely, Gayle C. "Florence Sabin: Distinguished Scientist." *More Than Petticoats: Remarkable Colorado Women*. Globe Pequot Press: Guilford, Connecticut, 2002.

Varnell, Jeanne. "Florence Rena Sabin." *Women of Consequence: The Colorado Women's Hall of Fame*. Johnson Books: Boulder, Colorado, 1999.

Index

About the Author

E. E. Duncan is an elementary school teacher in Denver Public Schools, with a specialty in gifted and talented education. She and her husband Robert have three young adult children, Katherine, Alexander and Christopher, as well as two cats and a frog. Growing up in Colorado, she learned to appreciate the beauty of the state and the individuals who contributed to its history. Ms. Duncan is the author of two previous biographies for young readers, *Ralph Carr: Defender of Japanese Americans* and *Felipe and Dolores Baca: Hispanic Pioneers*. She enjoys reading, writing, traveling, playing word games, and, of course, Colorado history.

MORE Now You Know Bios

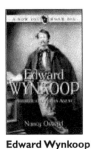

Edward Wynkoop
1831 – 1891
Soldier and Indian Agent
978-0-86541-184-5

John Denver
1943 – 1997
Singer, songwriter, world-known
performer, and humanitarian.
ISBN 978-086541-088-6

Dottie Lamm
1937 –
Former first lady of Colorado
and social activist.
ISBN 978-086541-085-5

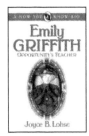

Emily Griffith
1868 – 1947
Educator and founder of Denver's
Emily Griffith Opportunity School.
ISBN 978-0-86541-077-0

José Dario Gallegos
1830 – 1883
Founder of San Luis,
oldest town in Colorado.
ISBN 978-0-86541-084-8

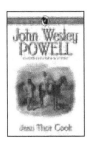

John Wesley Powell
1834 – 1902
Soldier, Explorer, Scientist. Led
the first exploration of the
Grand Canyon.
ISBN 978-0-86541-080-0

Justina Ford
1871 – 1952
The first African-American woman
to practice medicine in CO.
ISBN 978-0-86541-074-9

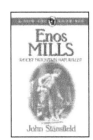

Enos Mills
1870 – 1922
The father of Rocky
Mountain National Park.
ISBN 978-0-86541-072-5

Martha Maxwell
1831 – 1881
Naturalist, innovative
taxidermist, museum builder.
ISBN 978-0-86541-075-6

Molly Brown
1867 – 1932
Heroine of the Titanic and
philanthropist.
ISBN 978-0-86541-081-7

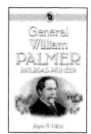

General William Palmer
1836 – 1909
Railroad pioneer, founder of
Colorado Springs, and
Civil War hero.
ISBN 978-0-86541-092-3

Chipeta
1843 – 1924
Ute peacemaker and wife
of Chief Ouray.
ISBN 978-0-86541-091-6

Mary Elitch Long
1856 – 1936
Founder of Elitch Gardens
Amusement Park in Denver, CO.
ISBN 978-0-86541-094-7

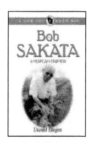

Bob Sakata
1926 –
American farmer and
community leader.
ISBN 978-0-86541-093-0

Susan Anderson
1870 – 1960
Pioneer mountain doctor
By Lydia Griffith
ISBN 978-0-86541-108-1

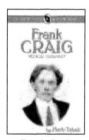

Frank Craig
1877 – 1914
Founded the Brotherly Relief Colony
for destitute consumptives, now the
Craig Rehabilitation Hospital.
ISBN 978-0-86541-092-3

Now You Know Bios are available at your local bookstore,
by calling 888.570.2663, and online at www.FilterPressBooks.com

Printed in the USA
CPSIA information can be obtained
at www.ICGtesting.com
JSHW040247110224
56836JS00013B/108

9 780865 411395